# green tea

greentea

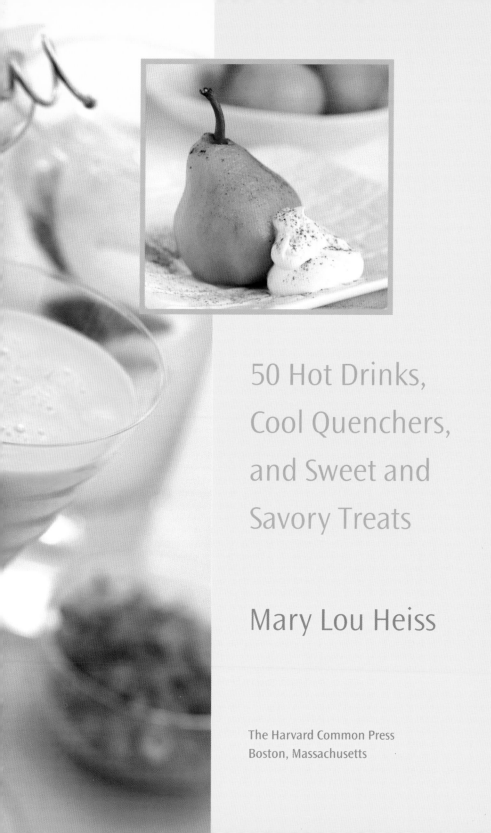

50 Hot Drinks,
Cool Quenchers,
and Sweet and
Savory Treats

Mary Lou Heiss

The Harvard Common Press
Boston, Massachusetts

*For Bob,*

*who never flinched when asked*

*to taste a new recipe:*

*You are the best cheerleader*

*a girl could wish for.*

The Harvard Common Press
535 Albany Street
Boston, Massachusetts 02118
www.harvardcommonpress.com

Printed in China
Printed on acid-free paper

*Library of Congress Cataloging-in-Publication Data*

Heiss, Mary Lou.
  Green tea : 50 hot drinks, cool quenchers, and sweet and savory treats / Mary Lou Heiss.
    p.  cm.
  Includes index.
  ISBN 1-55832-298-1 (hardcover : alk. paper)
  1. Cookery (Tea)   2. Green tea.   I. Title.
  TX817.T3H45 2006
  641.6'372—dc22

                                                     2005023807

  ISBN-13: 978-1-55832-298-1
  ISBN-10: 1-55832-298-1

Special bulk-order discounts are available on this and other Harvard Common Press books. Companies and organizations may purchase books for premiums or resale, or may arrange a custom edition, by contacting the Marketing Director at the address above.

10 9 8 7 6 5 4 3 2 1

*Book design by rlf design*

*Photographer: Richard Eskite; photo assistant: Brad Ryder; producer: Juliann Harvey; food styling: Andrea Lucich; food styling assistant: Caitlyn Hicks; prop styling: Carol Hacker*

# contents

# acknowledgments

Without the enthusiasm of The Harvard Common Press, this book would still be a dream. My sincere appreciation goes to Bruce Shaw, Valerie Cimino, Christine Corcoran Cox, and the rest of the talented team for all that they have done to make this book shine. Thanks also to Pam Hoenig for her early belief in this book, and to my agent, Lisa Ekus, for friendship and trust, the best part of the deal.

# introduction

In China and Japan, green tea is the fuel that drives and invigorates the daily lives of millions. From early morning until late at night, cups of fresh, fragrant green tea poured from steaming teapots provide an uplifting and relaxing break from the hectic pace of daily life. Much like Westerners and their beloved cups of coffee, many Asians never let their lidded cups of tea stray too far from sight.

Today, as in the past, housewives, students, workers, and travelers rely on the social pleasures of the local teahouse to provide a calm and meditative place for relaxing or catching up with a friend on the latest news. Accompanied by simple snacks, a modest cup of green tea soothes away the rough edges of the day and connects the drinker with social and cultural traditions of tea drinking that have endured for centuries.

The culture of green tea drinking in China and Japan goes beyond mere refreshment, as it is meant to engage and delight the senses through careful attention to both the preparation and the drinking of the tea. Much has been written by Chinese monks and Japanese Zen scholars to underscore the necessity for ritual in tea preparation. Additionally, writers and poets enthusiastically note the pleasures one can expect from drinking a cup of this tranquil, liquid jade.

Even with today's busy schedules, the classical nature of tea drinking in China and Japan is still respected. Tea drinking in Asia involves more than just the drinking of tea. The cups, water, room decorations, and sounds—or absence of sounds—are all important, and were deemed so in the Tang Dynasty. It is these elements that give tea its "classical nature." For the tea drinker, the sound of hot tea being poured from teapot to cup is reminiscent of pure, clean water gently coursing in a rocky stream. The translucent golden-green color of the tea in the hollow of a teacup should be visually pleasing, and the shape and design of the teacup should be engaging and feel good in the hand. The fragrance of the tea should stimulate the palate in anticipation of the flavor of the brew, which, upon tasting, should be delicate and fresh, reminding one of the cool, misty mountain of its origin.

Light in flavor, lower in caffeine than black tea or coffee, clean and contemporary in style, green tea is the beverage of choice for more than half the world's population. Twenty-somethings worldwide seem to find that the essence of green tea is more to their liking than black tea, and they are spreading the idea that green tea is "not your grandmother's cup of tea." Consumption of this pleasing beverage is spiraling upward in the West. Americans are challenging the popularity of traditional black tea by embracing the numerous styles of green tea available in specialty tea shops and from online tea merchants. Additionally, bottled green tea beverages are gaining a larger presence on grocers' shelves, and cafés and restaurants continue to add more choices of green tea. Green tea is the perfect, easy-to-brew, and delicious beverage of choice for a new generation of tea drinkers. It's healthful as well: medical research is finding that drinking three to four cups of green tea a day may help to reduce blood pressure, bolster immunity, protect skin from free-radical damage, and lower the incidence of cancer.

Hot or iced, plain or with spice or citrus, green tea is one of life's simple and satisfying pleasures. Adopt an Asian attitude and enjoy the many delights of this timeless beverage.

# green tea basics

$\mathcal{S}$econd only to water in consumption, green tea is a modern-day cultural icon in China, Japan, and South Korea. This staple of Asian life has spent 2,000 years earning its title as the world's oldest beverage.

A delicious cup of hot or iced green tea always starts with high-quality tea. Yielding 50 cups of tea per 4 ounces of dry leaves, exquisite green teas are an amazingly affordable luxury. Buy your tea from respected retailers or companies that you trust and that specialize in fine teas. Avoid inexpensive tea no matter how good a bargain it seems to be—it's not really a bargain, as it is guaranteed to make a disappointing brew.

## Loose-Leaf Tea

Leaf styles differ significantly between Chinese and Japanese green tea. Each is unique and reflects the practices and distinctive traditions of tea culture in these countries. While all tea bushes are of the same species of flowering evergreen, *Camellia sinensis,* it is the size of the leaf when it is plucked and the method of leaf manufacture that is responsible for the distinctions among green teas. Japanese green teas number fewer than a dozen choices, while it is thought that more than 8,000 distinctions of green tea are produced in the vast tea-producing regions of China.

In China, green tea is brewed from whole dried leaves. Elegant, clean, and fresh in flavor, the finest Chinese green teas are picked in the early spring and are prized for their artistically shaped, rolled or twisted hand-processed leaves. Chinese teas are rarely steamed, and can be machine shaped or traditionally hand processed in tea-firing pans or baskets, resulting in a dazzling assortment of shapes such as spirals and twists, pearls and balls, swords, tips and buds ("sparrow tongues"), and flat, pressed leaves.

Here at home, look in specialty tea shops or on the Internet (see Resource Guide, page 91) for fine-quality teas with lyrical names such as Bamboo Tips,

Mengding Mt. Snow Buds, Jade in the Clouds, Emerald Forest, Bubbling Spring, Ming Mei, Qi Mt. Dragon Whiskers, and Purple Bamboo. These names and distinctive leaf styles reflect China's ancient tea culture, and remind us that something as simple as a handful of tea leaves can offer the opportunity for dreamy reflection.

In Japan, green teas undergo a unique steaming process in their manufacture, which gives them a dark green color and minerally, vegetal flavor. The leaves are most commonly shaped by machine into long, delicate, uniform "needles." A passion for tea drinking seems built into the psyche of every Japanese man and woman. Sencha, the traditional tea consumed in vast quantities by Japanese people every day, is grown in several regions of Japan and has a fresh, vivid green color. Gyokuro ("jade dew") is the most treasured tea in Japan and is a beverage of elegance and refinement. Matcha, a silky-smooth, jewel-toned powdered green tea, is traditionally whisked into a frothy beverage during the Japanese tea ceremony. Matcha is also essential for infusing focused tea flavor and an attractive, vivid green color to desserts, fruit smoothies, and sauces. I use Kiri No Ne matcha or Hana No En matcha, both of which give excellent flavor and color.

In both China and Japan, the finest teas are harvested from early spring pickings, which begin in March or early April and continue into early May. The green tea season winds down by September, at which time the plants will be pruned and allowed to rest until the next harvest.

## Selecting Loose-Leaf Tea: Style and Flavor

There are many styles and satisfying flavors to discover as you explore the fascinating world of Chinese and Japanese green teas. As long as you know which style you are purchasing and you measure the leaves accordingly, you can use any green teas that you like in any of the recipes in this book. I have categorized some teas that you should look for to start you on your way. But remember, you will also discover many other wonderful teas from specialty vendors, so do not limit yourself to only these choices. Be sure to buy tea from shops that do a brisk business in green tea, so that you will get the freshest, most fragrant leaves available. Try to pinpoint the teas that are from the most current harvest and buy those. A reputable store will know this information and be proud of providing teas that are truly fresh.

**Light and fragrant style:** includes Dong Yang-Dong Bai, Huangshan Mao Feng, Jade in the Clouds, Mengding Mt. Snow Buds, Tai Ping Hou Kui.

**Medium and fresh style:** includes Bamboo Tips, Curled Dragon Silver Tips, Qi Mt. Dragon Whiskers, Ming Mei, Mist on the River, Mt. Tianmu, Szechuan Panda Tips.

**Full, earthy, toasty style:** includes Buddha's Peak, Dragonwell, Genmaicha, Young Hyson, Kukicha Yama, LuAn Melon Seeds, River of Clouds, Szechuan Crouching Tiger Tips.

**Full, minerally, spicy style:** includes Bi Lo Chun, Emerald Forest, Gunpowder, Gyokuro, Sencha.

## Measuring Loose-Leaf Green Tea

Green tea is lofty in volume relative to its weight and less straightforward to measure than black tea. The artistic configurations of green tea leaf styles and sizes—pearls, rings, twists, large flat leaves, tiny wiry leaves, and needle-thin leaves—present a measuring challenge. Generally, green tea can be grouped into three categories of leaf size: small, medium-size, and large. After a bit of practice using different teas, you will quickly begin to get the feel of how much tea to use when you encounter new and delicious types of tea.

The easiest way to measure green tea is with an inexpensive digital gram scale, available at kitchenware stores. In general, for hot tea use 2 grams of loose-leaf green tea for every 8 ounces of water; for cold tea use 3 grams for every 8 ounces. If you do not have one of these scales or do not wish to purchase one, grab your measuring spoons and follow the quantities suggested here.

**Small leaves, balls, and pearls:** 1 teaspoon tea per 8 ounces water. This type includes Bi Lo Chun, Bubbling Spring Rolled Green, Genmaicha, Gunpowder, Gyokuro, Hyson, Jasmine Pearls, Sencha, and Szechuan Crouching Tiger Tips.

**Medium-size leaves:** 1½ slightly rounded teaspoons tea per 8 ounces water. This type includes Bamboo Tips (Sparrow Tongue), Buddha's Peak, Dong Yang-Dong Bai, Dragonwell, Genmaicha, Mengding Mt. Snow Buds (Sparrow Tongue), Ming Mei, Mt. Tianmu, and Sencha.

**Large leaves:** 1 tablespoon tea per 8 ounces water. This type includes Curled Dragon Silver Tips, Huangshan Mao Feng, LuAn Melon Seeds, Mist on the River, Nine Dragons, River of Clouds, and Tai Ping Hou Kui.

## Tea Bags

Tea bags offer a convenient and easy way to enjoy a cup of tea when it is just not possible to brew a pot of loose-leaf tea. Several companies package excellent green tea in tea bags, and these tea bags will give you good flavor, not the dreaded bitterness of cheap-quality tea found in many tea bags. While I still recommend brewing loose-leaf tea whenever possible, quality tea bags will work well in nearly every recipe in this book.

When using tea bags to brew hot tea, use 1 tea bag per 8 ounces of water. Keep your ratio of tea to water constant and watch your brewing time very closely. Tea bags contain very finely cut or broken leaves that will brew a stronger, and sometimes more astringent, cup of tea than loose-leaf tea. Be on the lookout for "tea sachets," gauzy fabric pouches filled with whole-leaf teas. These soft-sided, slightly triangular pouches are much larger than tea bags and offer you the ease of a tea bag with more of the flavor of loose-leaf tea.

## Water

In the eighth-century Tang Dynasty, an aesthete and intellectual named Lu Yu wrote the first treatise on properly attending to the ritual appreciation of tea brewing. This book, *The Classic of Tea,* is still significant to tea culture in China today. Lu Yu advised: "On the question of what water to use, I would suggest that tea made from mountain streams is best, river water is all right, but well water is quite inferior." Today, this translates into using the freshest, purest water you can find. Tea requires pure, sweet water to produce the best flavor— I strongly recommend bottled water if your tap water has off flavors from algae, heavy minerals, old plumbing, or chemical treatments such as chlorine.

## Tea-Brewing Equipment

Asian tea drinkers drop tea leaves directly into the bottom of the teapot and allow the leaves to unfurl without restriction. Tea balls, mesh teaspoons, and other pieces of English-style black-tea-brewing paraphernalia are not appropriate for larger, intricately shaped green tea leaves, although you can use the small-handled tea strainers that sit atop individual cups. The best approach is to select a teapot that has a removable stainless steel mesh or nylon tea infuser, which allows you to quickly remove the tea leaves from the brew to prevent over-steeping and makes it easy to re-infuse the next pot. Also, look for single-serving-size mesh tea infusers that fit into your favorite mug. These, too, will allow green tea leaves to unfurl without restriction. These handy infusers are made of very fine stainless steel mesh and have little handles for

# classic hot green tea

This master recipe can be scaled up or down to serve as many as you like, as long as you keep the proportion of water to tea in balance. **Makes 2 cups**

2 cups fresh, cold water

1 tablespoon (4 grams) medium-size loose-leaf green tea or 2 green tea bags

**1.** Put the water in a kettle and heat to 175° to 180°F. Or bring the water to a boil, then remove the kettle from the heat, prop open or remove the lid, and let the water sit for 1 minute.

**2.** Place the tea leaves or tea bags into the infuser of a small ceramic, glass, or clay teapot, or place the tea directly into the teapot if there is a built-in strainer in the spout. If your teapot does not have an infuser or strainer, you can use a hand-held strainer placed over your cups to catch the tea leaves. Pour the heated water over the tea, put the lid back on, and steep for 2 minutes.

**3.** Remove the infuser from the teapot and pour the tea into teacups. Serve hot, preferably without milk or sugar.

easy removal from your cup. (The tightly woven mesh screening will ensure that all the particles of tea leaves, flowers, spices, etc., will be captured in the strainer.) The infuser nestles into the cup and allows plenty of room for loose-leaf tea to float and unfurl. With these infusers, it is as easy to use loose-leaf tea as it is to use a tea bag. Always cover your tea-brewing cup, as green tea brews best when covered.

## Temperature and Brewing Time

Asian methods of brewing green tea differ in every way possible from English methods of brewing black tea. Correct water temperature is essential for brewing delicate green teas—water that is too hot will scorch the leaves and create bitterness. In China, people observe the pot of tea water while it is heating; for green tea, they remove it from the heat when a pillar of steam begins to rise up from the surface of the water. At this point, the water is 175° to 180°F, the ideal temperature for infusing green tea leaves. Asians also give green tea a short brewing time of two minutes, the best infusion time for most green tea. Some green teas are best with an infusion time even shorter than two minutes. You can experiment, but be aware that a longer brewing time is not beneficial to the flavor of green tea, as more time will encourage overextraction and the tea will become sour tasting.

## Re-Infusing Tea Leaves

Unlike black teas, most Chinese and Japanese green teas can be successfully re-infused two or three times, increasing the yield of 50 cups of tea per 4 ounces of dried leaf to double or triple that figure. In fact, Asian tea-drinking custom holds that green teas do not release their most delicate, precious flavors until the second or third infusion. Try it for yourself and see—simply re-introduce more hot water to the tea leaves after you brew the first pot and brew for two minutes. When re-infusing Chinese green teas, increase the water temperature slightly for each additional re-infusion, and for Japanese teas, reduce the water temperature slightly each time. These additional infusions will further "open up" the tea leaf, yielding subtly different flavors from one infusion to the next. In Chinese teahouses, waiters stroll around with large, well-worn kettles of hot water, looking out for customers who signal that they need more water by tapping their index and middle fingers on the table.

# Double Infusions

Many recipes in this book call for first infusing spices or herbs in the same hot water that is then used to brew the green tea. If you have two 6-cup tea-pots, you can simply use those to do this. But if not, a standard 4-cup heat-proof measuring cup will work beautifully for the first infusion.

And speaking of spices, for the best flavor, use whole spices and crush them as directed in the recipes. Ground spices are generally not good substi-tutes in tea infusions. Use fresh herbs whenever possible. They have delicate flavors that are subtler than the flavors of dried herbs. Flowers such as rose-buds, chamomile, and chrysanthemum are best used dried.

# Storing Brewed Tea

Hot tea should be served immediately, of course. Stored in a pitcher with a lid, chilled green tea will keep in your refrigerator for up to two days. Chilled green tea kept any longer acquires an off taste that changes the flavor, making it metallic and unpleasant. When chilled green tea is mixed with other ingre-dients, as in the iced tea recipes on pages 38 to 53, the process is slowed down, but I do not recommend storing plain green tea for longer than two days.

# Healthful Benefits of Green Tea

Green tea and good health have a wellness association for Asians, and in-creasingly for Westerners, that goes beyond mere folk wisdom or popular be-lief. For centuries, Asians have believed in the healthful benefits of drinking green tea. Today, researchers in the West are scrutinizing the complex chemi-cal structure of these simple leaves, and they are compiling an impressive list of healthful benefits that point to the fact that the regular drinking of green tea contributes to maintaining human health.

According to the Beltsville Human Nutrition Research Center, a research arm of the USDA, green tea contains four powerful flavonoid polyphenol com-pounds (antioxidants) known as catechins. It is these catechin compounds—EC, ECG, EGC, and EGCG—that are the healthful antioxidant components of green tea. The role of antioxidants as disease fighters involves protecting human cells from the attack of cancer-causing free radical cells found in the human body. Antioxidants do this by preventing tumor-generating conditions from occurring in advance of the potential onset of disease. Additionally,

# classic iced green tea

Use this basic recipe for all the iced tea, smoothie, and cocktail recipes in later chapters. For iced green tea, I recommend that you use 6 grams of loose-leaf tea (instead of the 4 grams that I suggest for hot green tea) per 16 ounces of water. Green tea, unlike black tea, does not respond well to double-strength brewing, but the flavor of iced green tea does benefit from using 50 percent more leaves. When using tea bags, use 3 bags instead of 2.

**Makes 2 cups**

2 cups fresh, cold water

4½ teaspoons (6 grams) medium-size
  loose-leaf green tea or 3 green
  tea bags

**1.** Put the water in a kettle and heat to 175° to 180°F. Or bring the water to a boil, then remove the kettle from the heat, prop open or remove the lid, and let the water sit for 1 minute.

**2.** Place the tea leaves or tea bags into the infuser of a small ceramic, glass, or clay teapot, or place the tea directly into the teapot if there is a built-in strainer in the spout. If your teapot does not have an infuser or strainer, you can use a hand-held strainer placed over your cups to catch the tea leaves. Pour the heated water over the tea, put the lid back on, and steep for 2 minutes.

**3.** Remove the infuser from the teapot and set the teapot aside to cool, or strain the tea into a heatproof container. When the tea has cooled, pour the tea into a glass container and place it in the refrigerator to chill. Serve in tall glasses over ice.

catechins may prove to be beneficial for nontoxic treatment of existing cancers. For example, testing by the Mayo Clinic has discovered that EGCG helps kill leukemia cells by interrupting the nourishing blood flow to the cancer cells, leaving the cancer cells to wither and die.

Studies at the University of Kansas, Lawrence, have concluded that EGCG, tea's most abundant antioxidant catechin, is 100 times more potent than vitamin C and 25 times more potent than vitamin E when it comes to helping to protect cells and their DNA from damage thought to be linked to cancer and heart disease. Research at Tufts University suggests that one 6-ounce cup of tea contains approximately 235 milligrams of catechins, compared to 178 grams found in a medium-size apple. In Japan, another group of catechins, the gallate group, is being studied regarding its ability to reduce body fat by affecting the way that sugar is processed and held by fat-storing cells.

Ongoing clinical studies indicate that green tea has been shown to strengthen blood vessels, decrease bad LDL cholesterol levels in the blood, reduce the occurrence of blood clots, aid digestion, lower blood pressure, and stabilize blood sugar. The National Cancer Institute is measuring green tea's role in the prevention of many cancers, including cancer of the bladder, breast, colon, esophagus, liver, lung, and stomach. While researchers have yet to determine exactly how much green tea one needs to consume every day to obtain these health benefits, dietary studies with volunteers seem to indicate that it is necessary to drink four to five cups a day.

The many statistical reports that list the milligram content of caffeine present in 8-ounce cups of brewed tea and coffee vary greatly, and this brings the particulars of testing for caffeine into question. Without knowing if the testing was conducted in a similar manner with identical products, it is impossible to know which information is correct. Many factors play a role in determining the caffeine content of tea. These include the variety of tea, the size and age of the leaves when picked, whole leaf tea versus tea from tea bags, the method of brewing, and the measurement used. However, all of this analysis does point to a consistent pattern, which is that cup for cup, green tea usually contains less caffeine than black tea (8 to 16 milligrams versus 25 to 110 milligrams) and significantly less caffeine than an 8-ounce cup of coffee, which contains about 128 milligrams.

What happy good fortune it is that green tea, which is so delicious and such a snap to brew, seems to have only healthy attributes. Make the switch to green tea and you will be depositing credits into your healthy-lifestyle bank account, from which you will earn valuable dividends throughout your long life.

hot green tea

*L*egions of tea drinkers around the world count on the stimulation and mildly energizing effects of steaming hot green tea to wake them up and keep them going throughout the day. Green tea is always pleasing when served plain and hot, but in these recipes you will find fruit, spice, and herbal flavors that are designed to complement green tea's subtle nuances.

---

Invigorating and Spicy Green Tea • Soothing and Relaxing Green Tea • Green Tea with Indian Chai Spices • Chrysanthemum Harmony Green Tea • Chamomile Blossom–Honey Green Tea • Fruity Green Tea "Hot Toddy" • White Ginger and Spearmint Green Tea • Lemongrass, Fennel, and Peppermint Green Tea • Cinnamon–Star Anise Green Tea • Green Tea with Rosebuds and Chrysanthemum Flowers • Moroccan Mint Green Tea • Genmaicha with Maple and Cinnamon • Pucker-Up Lemon Green Tea

# invigorating and spicy green tea

2 tablespoons (8 grams) medium-size loose-leaf green tea or 4 green tea bags

9 freshly cracked green or white cardamom pods

9 whole white peppercorns

One 3-inch piece cinnamon stick

4 cups boiling water

Serves 2 to 4

The bold flavors of these warm spices are tamed a bit so as to add a subtle flavor that imparts a nice bit of underlying heat without overpowering the delicacy of the tea. For the best aromatics, use soft, true Ceylon cinnamon, which can be identified by sticks that are lightweight, brittle, and flaky. Avoid the hard, woody variety of cinnamon, which is actually cassia. Cassia is the bark of a tree in the laurel family, and while it is commonly sold in the United States as cinnamon, it lacks the flavor and aroma of true Ceylon cinnamon.

1. Put the tea leaves or tea bags into a pre-warmed large teapot and set aside.

2. Place the spices in a 4-cup heatproof measuring cup and add the boiling water. Stir to mix, then let the spices infuse for 2 minutes.

3. Quickly pour the infusion into the teapot, straining carefully to prevent the spices from going into the teapot. Steep the tea in the spice infusion for an additional 2 minutes.

4. Strain the brewed tea into teacups and serve immediately.

# soothing and relaxing green tea

This aromatic tea has been known to bring relaxation and a sense of calm to all who drink it. It is an excellent choice for a lazy Sunday morning spent catching up with the newspaper or for winding down after a long walk.

1. Put the tea leaves or tea bags into a pre-warmed large teapot and set aside.

2. Place the lemon zest and ginger in a 4-cup heatproof measuring cup and add the boiling water. Using the back of a spoon, press the pieces of ginger against the side of the measuring cup to release their juice, then let them infuse for 2 minutes.

3. Quickly pour the infusion into the teapot, straining carefully to prevent the spices from going into the teapot. Steep the tea in the spice infusion for an additional 2 minutes.

4. Add a touch of sugar or honey if desired. Strain the brewed tea into teacups and serve immediately.

2 tablespoons (8 grams) medium-size loose-leaf green tea or 4 green tea bags

2 teaspoons lemon zest

5 slices peeled fresh ginger, coarsely chopped

4 cups boiling water

Sugar or honey to taste (optional)

Serves 2 to 4

The simplest and fastest way to zest citrus fruit is to use a microplane grater. It is incredibly sharp, and with virtually no effort it magically produces a bounty of aromatic citrus zest. Create your own variation to this recipe by using orange, lime, or tangerine zest.

# green tea with indian chai spices

2 tablespoons (8 grams)
medium-size loose-leaf
green tea or 4 green
tea bags

4 whole white cardamom
pods

4 whole allspice berries

6 whole black peppercorns

2 whole star anise

One 2-inch piece
cinnamon stick

4 cups boiling water

1 teaspoon sugar

Serves 2 to 4

Classic Indian chai is prepared with black tea, fragrant spices, milk, and sugar. First, the tea and spices are simmered in water, then milk and sugar are added, and the brew is simmered again. The region of India where chai reigns supreme is in the north, and in this land of fragrant spices, *masala chaiwallas* (tea vendors) proudly develop their own versions of this beverage. My interpretation uses green tea and a global blend of spices. Hold the milk, but do add sugar.

**1.** Put the tea leaves or tea bags into a pre-warmed large teapot and set aside.

**2.** Crack open the cardamom pods using a mortar and pestle. Discard the empty pods, but keep the tiny black seeds. Add the remaining spices to the mortar and crush all into medium-size pieces. Put the spices into a 4-cup heatproof measuring cup and add the boiling water. Stir to mix, then let the spices infuse for 2 minutes.

**3.** Quickly pour the infusion into the teapot, straining carefully to prevent the spices from going into the teapot. Steep the tea in the spice infusion for 2 minutes.

**4.** Add the sugar to the teapot and stir to dissolve. Strain the brewed tea into teacups and serve immediately.

# chrysanthemum harmony green tea

2 tablespoons (8 grams) medium-size loose-leaf green tea or 4 green tea bags

3 whole green or white cardamom pods

8 whole white peppercorns

8 white chrysanthemum flowers

4 cups boiling water

Serves 2 to 4

While staying in a hotel nestled atop the craggy pinnacles of China's otherworldly Huangshan Mountains, I noticed tiny white chrysanthemum blossoms floating lazily in my pot of tea. I learned that in the green tea–producing province of Anhui, Chinese tea drinkers favor these fragrant flowers (along with jasmine and lychee blossoms and tiny rosebuds) for their sweet aroma and delicate flavor and the pleasing way that they float in the cup. My version has aromatic spices along with the sweetness of the chrysanthemum blossoms. Look for chrysanthemum flowers in Asian markets or online at www.cooksshophere.com.

**1.** Put the tea leaves or tea bags into a pre-warmed large teapot and set aside.

**2.** Crack open the cardamom pods using a mortar and pestle. Discard the empty pods, but keep the tiny black seeds. Put the cardamom seeds, white peppercorns, and chrysanthemum flowers into a 4-cup heatproof measuring cup and add the boiling water. Stir to mix, then let the blossoms and spices infuse for 4 minutes.

**3.** Quickly pour the infusion into the teapot, straining carefully to prevent the spices from going into the teapot. Steep the tea in the spice infusion for 2 minutes.

**4.** Strain the brewed tea into teacups and serve immediately.

# chamomile blossom–honey green tea

Chamomile is a favorite of European tea drinkers, who love its soothing nature and delicious, apple-like scent. When purchasing chamomile tea bags, look for the Pompadour brand from Germany or the Twinings brand from England. It is also easy to grow chamomile in your garden.

2 tablespoons (8 grams) medium-size loose-leaf green tea or 4 green tea bags

2 tablespoons loose chamomile flowers or 2 chamomile tea bags

4 cups boiling water

4 teaspoons mild floral honey, such as tupelo, lavender, or raspberry

Serves 2 to 4

**1.** Put the green tea leaves or tea bags into a pre-warmed large teapot and set aside.

**2.** Put the chamomile flowers into a 4-cup heatproof measuring cup and add the boiling water. Stir to mix, then let the flowers infuse for 2 minutes.

**3.** Quickly pour the infusion into the teapot, straining carefully to prevent the flowers from going into the teapot. Steep the tea in the chamomile infusion for 2 minutes.

**4.** Add the honey to the pot and stir to dissolve. Strain the brewed tea into teacups and serve immediately.

If you use tea bags for both the green tea and the chamomile, be sure to steep the chamomile in the boiling water first for 2 minutes, then add the green tea and steep 2 minutes longer. Remove the tea bags and press them gently against the side of the teapot to drain.

# fruity green tea "hot toddy"

Besides being a wonderful hot tea, this also makes a refreshing and delicious everyday iced beverage. Feel free to "spike" the hot version with dark rum and vodka or brandy and orange liqueur when you have friends over for a festive holiday party. For the best flavor, buy all-natural bottled pear and pineapple juices, not overly sweetened, thin-on-flavor canned juice drinks. These days you don't have to juice your own fruit to get fresh, natural, flavorful juice, but every step you take closer to "fresh squeezed" adds another element of delicious—and nutritious—flavor.

1 tablespoon (4 grams) medium-size loose-leaf green tea or 2 green tea bags

1 cup orange juice

1 cup natural pear juice or nectar

1 cup pineapple juice

4 orange slices, halved

4 lemon slices, halved

2 cups water, boiled and cooled to 175° to 180°F

3 tablespoons caramel syrup

2 lemon slices, cut into quarters

Serves 4

1. Put the tea leaves or tea bags into a pre-warmed teapot and set aside.

2. Put the orange, pear, and pineapple juices into a medium-size saucepan and add the fruit slices. Carefully bring the contents to a simmer over low heat.

3. Add the water to the tea in the teapot and steep for 2 minutes.

4. Strain the brewed tea into the juice mixture and bring the heat back to a simmer. Add the caramel syrup and mix well. Discard the fruit slices.

5. Ladle the hot tea into teacups or mugs and garnish each with 2 pieces of lemon. Serve immediately.

Caramel syrup is a handy sugar syrup to have in the kitchen for all sorts of uses. If you cannot locate it, substitute turbinado or light muscovado brown sugar.

# white ginger and spearmint green tea

2 tablespoons (8 grams) medium-size loose-leaf green tea or 4 green tea bags

3 tablespoons peeled and finely chopped fresh ginger

½ cup very tightly packed fresh mint leaves or ¼ teaspoon finely crushed dried spearmint

4 cups boiling water

Serves 2 to 4

**You can make this tea using both green tea and spearmint tea bags. Be sure to let the water cool to 175° to 180°F, then put both types of tea bags into the teapot and infuse them together for 2 minutes. Remove the tea bags and press them gently against the side of the teapot to drain.**

Fresh ginger and spearmint complement each other in a wonderfully sassy way and make this tea, whether hot or iced, a welcome refreshment at any time of day. Spearmint adds such a fresh, clean favor to beverages that I use it often and in abundance. If you grow fresh spearmint in your garden or in a patio pot, then you know what a treat it is to be able to clip fistfuls of it on demand. In the market, fresh mint is always available, and while it may be labeled plain "mint" and not specifically "spearmint," it will no doubt be just as fragrant and delicious.

**1.** Put the tea leaves or tea bags into a pre-warmed large teapot and set aside.

**2.** Put the ginger and mint into a 4-cup heat-proof measuring cup and add the boiling water. Stir to mix, then infuse for 2 minutes.

**3.** Quickly pour the infusion into the teapot, straining carefully to keep the ginger and mint from going into the teapot. Steep the tea in the spice infusion for 2 minutes.

**4.** Strain the brewed tea into teacups and serve immediately.

# lemongrass, fennel, and peppermint green tea

Lemongrass and fennel might seem to be an odd couple, but they go together quite well in this tongue-tingling tea. The peppermint backs up the fennel and gives this tea a substantial flavor that is feisty enough to cap off a savory evening meal. Drink this tea when you need a whole-body lift or after a vigorous workout.

2 tablespoons (8 grams) medium-size loose-leaf green tea or 4 green tea bags

1 teaspoon whole fennel seeds

16 thin slices fresh lemongrass

2 teaspoons finely crushed dried peppermint

4 cups boiling water

Serves 2 to 4

**1.** Put the tea leaves or tea bags into a prewarmed large teapot and set aside.

**2.** Put the fennel seeds, lemongrass, and peppermint into a 4-cup heatproof measuring cup and add the boiling water. Stir to mix, then infuse for 2 minutes.

**3.** Quickly pour the infusion into the teapot, straining carefully to keep the fennel, lemongrass, and peppermint from going into the teapot. Steep the tea in the spice infusion for 2 minutes.

**4.** Strain the brewed tea into teacups and serve immediately.

You can make this tea using both green tea and peppermint tea bags. Be sure to let the water cool to 175° to 180°F, then put both types of tea bags into the teapot and infuse them together for 2 minutes. Remove the tea bags and press them gently against the side of the teapot to drain.

29

# cinnamon–star anise green tea

2 tablespoons (8 grams) medium-size loose-leaf green tea or 4 green tea bags

One 5-inch cinnamon stick, broken into pieces

8 whole star anise or 1½ tablespoons broken star anise pieces

4 cups boiling water

Serves 2 to 4

Cinnamon and star anise are wonderful partners in this heady, aromatic brew. Star anise is actually the fruit of a small evergreen tree in the magnolia family that is found in China and Vietnam. Known in China as *bah-jyao*, "eight points," it gets its name from the (usually) eight irregular points that create its distinctive shape. Each point contains a shiny brown seed that adds to the spicy, woodsy fragrance and flavor. Serve big mugs of this tea to chase away the frosty bite of a brisk fall morning, or after a vigorous afternoon of snowshoeing or cross-country skiing. It is a wonderful tea to serve with homemade baked goodies such as muffins or scones.

**1.** Put the tea leaves or tea bags into a pre-warmed large teapot and set aside.

**2.** Put the cinnamon and star anise pieces into a 4-cup heatproof measuring cup and add the boiling water. Stir to mix, then infuse for 2 minutes.

**3.** Quickly pour the infusion into the teapot, straining carefully to keep the cinnamon and star anise from going into the teapot. Steep the tea in the spice infusion for 2 minutes.

**4.** Strain the brewed tea into teacups and serve immediately.

# green tea with rosebuds and chrysanthemum flowers

Chinese hosts love to regale foreign visitors with cups of sweet, floral teas such as chrysanthemum, jasmine, lychee, osmanthus, or rose. In Chinese teahouses, customers indulge in these perfumed teas, elixirs accompanied by little plates of nuts, sunflower seeds, sesame seed candies, sweet bean buns, and juicy pieces of fresh fruit. Aromatic floral teas are often served with a small amount of white or brown rock sugar crystals placed in the bottom of each teacup, where they dissolve slowly, making each sip sweeter than the last. Look for dried flowers and rock sugar at Asian or specialty food stores or online at www.cooksshophere.com.

2 tablespoons (8 grams) medium-size loose-leaf green tea or 4 green tea bags

¼ cup miniature dried rosebuds

12 dried chrysanthemum flowers

4 cups water, boiled and cooled to 175° to 180°F

4 teaspoons brown or white rock sugar crystals

Serves 2 to 4

1. Put the tea leaves or tea bags into a pre-warmed large teapot and set aside.

2. Put the rosebuds and chrysanthemum flowers into a 4-cup heatproof measuring cup and add the water. Stir to mix, then infuse for 2 minutes.

3. Quickly pour the infusion into the teapot, straining carefully to keep the rosebuds and chrysanthemum flowers from going into the teapot. Steep the tea in the floral infusion for 2 minutes.

4. Strain the brewed tea into teacups and add a teaspoon of rock sugar crystals to each cup. Serve immediately.

# moroccan mint green tea

4 teaspoons (8 grams)
  Pinhead Gunpowder tea
  or 4 Gunpowder tea bags

1 cup very tightly packed
  fresh mint leaves

2 tablespoons brown or
  white rock sugar crystals

4 cups water, boiled and
  cooled to 175° to 180°F

Serves 2 to 4

In Morocco, exotically bejeweled teapots with long, curved spouts dispense hot mint tea into tall, thin, colorful tea glasses throughout the afternoon and evening. To re-create the flavor you must use Gunpowder tea, a Chinese green tea that is famous for its tightly rolled shape, and fresh mint. For authentic Moroccan-style tea you must put the Gunpowder tea into the teapot first, then add a handful of fresh mint leaves, followed by several large spoonfuls of sugar. Then the teapot must be filled with hot water until it nearly overflows. If you accompany this tea with a platter of delicacies such as baklava, fresh apricots, pistachios, and Turkish delight candy, you will be instantly transported to the crowded and mysterious streets of a Moroccan bazaar.

1. Put the tea leaves or tea bags into a large teapot. Pack in the fresh mint, then add the rock sugar crystals.

2. Add the water, stir gently, and cover the teapot. Steep the tea mixture for 2 minutes.

3. Strain the brewed tea into Moroccan-style tea glasses or teacups and serve immediately.

# genmaicha with maple and cinnamon

2 tablespoons (8 grams) medium-size loose-leaf Genmaicha or 4 Genmaicha tea bags

One 5-inch cinnamon stick, broken into pieces

2 tablespoons pure maple syrup

4 cups boiling water

Serves 2 to 4

You may substitute turbinado or light muscovado brown sugar for the maple syrup.

Genmaicha is a unique, much-loved Japanese tea that is a combination of Sencha green tea and miniature kernels of roasted and popped rice. Genmaicha has a pleasing roasted flavor and aroma that goes well with sweets such as butter cookies, shortbread, sesame seed cookies, and blondies. Also be sure to try this tea at breakfast, with walnut scones or bowls of steaming hot oatmeal. An American colleague who lives in Japan told me that her husband loves to have Genmaicha tea with American-style cinnamon toast for breakfast.

**1.** Put the tea leaves or tea bags into a prewarmed large teapot and set aside.

**2.** Place the cinnamon pieces and maple syrup in a 4-cup heatproof measuring cup and add the boiling water. Stir to mix, then let the cinnamon infuse for 2 minutes.

**3.** Quickly pour the infusion into the teapot, straining carefully to prevent the cinnamon from going into the teapot. Steep the tea in the spice infusion for an additional 2 minutes.

**4.** Strain the brewed tea into teacups and serve immediately.

# pucker-up lemon green tea

I love to make this tea really sing by adding a little extra lemon zest and a spoonful of sweet, golden honey. This is not a subtle tea, but it's a perfect flavor when you want to sharpen up and clear any lazy cobwebs from your mind. Just the aroma of this tea gives you advance warning of the energy lift coming your way. It is also an excellent palate refresher. Enjoy a cup with moist slices of homemade fruitcake or chewy oatmeal-raisin cookies.

2 tablespoons (8 grams) medium-size loose-leaf green tea or 4 green tea bags

1 teaspoon lemon zest

4 cups water, boiled and cooled to 175° to 180°F

2 teaspoons freshly squeezed lemon juice

Honey or sugar to taste

Serves 2 to 4

**1.** Put the tea leaves or tea bags and the lemon zest into a 4-cup heatproof glass measuring cup. Add the water and infuse for 2 minutes.

**2.** Quickly pour the infusion into a large teapot, straining carefully to prevent the lemon zest from going into the teapot. Add the lemon juice and a touch of honey or sugar to taste.

**3.** Pour the brewed tea into teacups and serve immediately.

iced green tea
and smoothies

*T*hese recipes emphasize green tea's versatility, so whether you drink iced tea year round or gravitate toward it when the mercury climbs, you'll be sure to find something you like. Iced tea is a snap to make and uses ingredients that you likely already have on hand. Experiment with different flavors and add sugar to taste to find your own iced tea heaven.

Smoothies offer a delicious choice for breakfast, a power-packed lunch, or a post-workout snack. Whether you make them smooth or chunky, juice based or creamy, it is almost impossible to run out of combinations to blend together to create these healthy beverages. For a protein-rich foundation, begin with yogurt, tofu, or soymilk, then add fresh fruit and juice. Green tea can be incorporated as brewed and cooled tea or as matcha powder. With such good ingredients, you really cannot go wrong—you will be concocting your own favorite recipes in no time.

---

Lemon Verbena and Peppermint Iced Green Tea • South-of-the-Border Watermelon Iced Green Tea • Fresh Lime and White Grape Iced Green Tea • Blushing Peach Iced Green Tea • Mango-Tango Iced Green Tea • Strawberry-Red Iced Green Tea • Johnny Appleseed Iced Green Tea • Pineapple-Ginger Iced Green Tea • Va-Va-Voom Mint Iced Green Tea • Jasmine Tea Limeade • In-the-Pink Iced Green Tea • Minty Green Tea Lemonade • Toasted Coconut Iced Green Tea • Green Tea, Pear, and Almond Horchata • Pineapple-Apricot Green Tea Smoothie • Cherry Green Tea Smoothie • Green Tea Apricot-Mango Smoothie • No-Moo Red-on-Red Green Tea Smoothie • Green Tea, Watermelon, and Pear Smoothie • Green Tea, Guava, and Pineapple Smoothie • Green Tea Banana Split Smoothie

# lemon verbena and peppermint iced green tea

4 teaspoons freshly
squeezed lemon juice

¼ cup tightly packed fresh
lemon verbena leaves or
4 heaping tablespoons
whole-leaf dried lemon
verbena

12 large whole fresh mint
leaves or ¼ teaspoon
finely crushed dried
peppermint

2 cups boiling water

2 cups chilled green tea

Sugar to taste (optional)

Ice cubes

Lemon slices and sugar,
for garnish

Serves 2 to 4

I love the crisp flavor and aroma of lemon verbena, so I make sure to have a thick patch of it growing in my garden every summer. Its fragrance is so refreshing on a hot and humid summer day. At summer's end I uproot the plants and, after shaking off the dirt, I hang them upside-down in a sheltered place to dry. This ensures that I can enjoy the aroma and flavor of this delightful herb all winter long.

**1.** Put the lemon juice, lemon verbena, and mint into a 4-cup heatproof measuring cup. Add the boiling water and infuse for 2 minutes. Strain the infusion into another heatproof container and allow to cool. Refrigerate until well chilled.

**2.** Combine the lemon-herb infusion with the chilled green tea in a medium-size pitcher. If desired, add a touch of sugar and stir to dissolve.

**3.** Pour the tea mixture into glasses filled with ice and garnish with lemon slices dredged in sugar. Serve immediately.

# south-of-the-border watermelon iced green tea

South of Mexico City in the agricultural region of Puebla, I fell in love with the colorful and beguiling local beverages known as *aguas frescas*. These simple, refreshing fruit drinks are available at street-corner fruit stands and are made from a bounty of ripe, in-season local fruits. They inspired this thirst-quenching iced tea flavored with watermelon, cinnamon, and brown sugar. This lively, vivid pink treat makes perfect use of summer's watermelon bounty.

3 cups chopped seedless watermelon

1 cup chilled green tea

1 cup chilled cream soda

⅛ teaspoon ground cinnamon

1 teaspoon light brown sugar

Ice cubes

Two to four 5-inch-long cinnamon sticks, for garnish

Serves 2 to 4

**1.** Put all of the ingredients except the ice cubes and cinnamon sticks into a blender and blend on medium speed for 2 minutes.

**2.** Pour the tea mixture into old-fashioned glasses filled with ice. Stand a cinnamon stick up in each glass and serve immediately.

# fresh lime and white grape iced green tea

2 cups chilled green tea

2 cups chilled white grape juice

6 tablespoons freshly squeezed lime juice

Sugar to taste (optional)

Ice cubes

Small lime wedges or lime slices, for garnish

Serves 2 to 4

This refreshing drink is based on the icy, pucker-up limeades I loved when I was a child. This iced tea is, of course, less sugary, and the flavor has a grown-up, polished style. It hits the spot when the temperature soars and it is time to retreat from the yard to a shady spot on the porch. When company is coming or you just want a dressier presentation, run a piece of cut lime around the rim of each glass and quickly dip the rim in a saucer of sugar to create a thin crust. Add a bamboo skewer decorated with lime slices and serve frosty cold.

**1.** Put the green tea, grape juice, and lime juice into a medium-size pitcher and stir well. Add sugar if desired.

**2.** Pour the tea mixture into glasses filled with ice. In each glass, float 4 lime wedges or add a skewer threaded with lime slices.

# blushing peach iced green tea

1 cup chilled green tea

1 cup chilled peach juice

1 cup chilled ginger ale

2 tablespoons black currant syrup

Ice cubes

Whole fresh raspberries or sprigs of fresh mint, for garnish

Serves 2 to 4

Delicate in color and flavor, this refreshing iced tea is right at home at the fanciest of luncheons. The ginger ale harmonizes deliciously with the peach juice and the green tea. Add a touch of color by garnishing with a sprig of fresh mint, or by floating a few fresh raspberries in each glass.

**1.** Put all of the ingredients except the ice cubes and raspberries or mint into a medium-size pitcher and stir well to combine.

**2.** Pour the tea mixture into tall glasses filled with ice. Float a few fresh raspberries in each glass, or add a sprig of mint to each glass, and serve immediately.

For a *très élégant* libation for special occasions, turn this drink into a cocktail variation of a Kir Royale by substituting Champagne or sparkling wine for the ginger ale and cassis (black currant liqueur) for the black currant syrup.

# mango-tango iced green tea

Tropical fruits and juicy peaches flavor this luscious Caribbean-inspired treat. This iced tea provides a lift anytime you feel the urge for an island paradise pick-me-up. For added zip, grate a little fresh ginger and add it to the brew.

**1.** Put all of the ingredients except the ice cubes and mint into a blender and blend for 2 minutes.

**2.** Pour the tea mixture into tall glasses filled with ice. Garnish with fresh mint sprigs and serve immediately.

1½ cups chilled green tea

¾ cup chilled mango puree

¾ cup chilled peach juice

1 cup chilled pineapple juice

1 teaspoon freshly squeezed lemon juice

Ice cubes

Sprigs of fresh mint, for garnish

Serves 2 to 4

Add a touch of dark rum if you really want to imagine that you are kicking back in the shade of the palm trees.

# strawberry-red iced green tea

Strawberries are a perfect foil for the slight astringency of green tea, and they give this iced tea a bewitching deep red color and a very pleasing flavor. In fact, should you find yourself with an abundance of fresh strawberries, you can simply wash, hull, and puree several handfuls in a blender with a little sugar and water to use instead of the frozen mix. The addition of the fruit syrup underscores and enlivens the strawberry flavor; black currant syrup in particular creates a special kind of chemistry in this combination.

One 10-ounce can frozen strawberry daiquiri mix (non-alcoholic), diluted with 1 can cold water

2 cups chilled green tea

2 tablespoons black currant, strawberry, or raspberry syrup

Ice cubes

Strawberries and sugar, for garnish

Serves 2 to 4

**1.** Put the strawberry daiquiri mixture into a medium-size pitcher and stir until thawed and blended. Add the chilled green tea and fruit syrup and mix thoroughly.

**2.** Pour the tea mixture into tall glasses filled with ice.

**3.** Make a garnish for each glass by sliding 3 strawberries onto a skewer, then rolling the skewer in sugar. Place 1 skewer in each glass and serve immediately.

# johnny appleseed
# iced green tea

1 cup chilled green tea

1 cup chilled unfiltered
apple cider

Four 2-inch strips lemon
peel

1½ cups very fizzy chilled
root beer

Ice cubes

Serves 2 to 4

By mid-October, fall in New England is well under way. Maple trees blanket the hillsides in a glorious tapestry of soft orange, rich yellow, and vibrant red. In the golden warmth of late afternoon, when the wind is right, I can smell the wafting aroma of apples as they are being pressed into fresh cider at the orchard on the ridge behind my house. For this recipe, search out cloudy, unfiltered, true farmstand cider, brimming with intense apple flavor.

**1.** Mix the chilled green tea with the apple cider in a medium-size pitcher. Add the lemon peel to the pitcher and stir. Add the root beer to the pitcher and blend thoroughly.

**2.** Pour the tea mixture into tall glasses filled with ice and serve immediately.

If you are fortunate
enough to find it,
freshly pressed pear
cider will also work
beautifully here.

# pineapple-ginger iced green tea

This chartreuse-hued iced tea is very satisfying. Pineapple juice is a popular drink in southwestern China and across Southeast Asia—hence my inspiration for pairing it with green tea. Fizzy ginger ale cuts the sweetness just a bit. Feel free to substitute sharp ginger beer if you want a bolder ginger taste. Use the best all-natural pineapple juice you can find—the pulpier the better! Or better yet, trim and puree a fresh, ripe pineapple in a blender for the ultimate pineapple flavor. Strain the juice or not, depending on your preference.

1 cup chilled green tea

2 cups chilled pineapple juice

1 cup very fizzy chilled ginger ale

Ice cubes

Serves 4

**1.** Mix the chilled green tea with the pineapple juice in a medium-size pitcher. Stir well. Add the ginger ale to the pitcher and blend thoroughly.

**2.** Pour the tea mixture into tall glasses filled with ice and serve immediately.

# va-va-voom mint iced green tea

4 cups chilled green tea

¼ cup green mint syrup

¼ cup freshly squeezed
  lemon juice

Cracked ice

Sprigs of fresh mint and
  lemon slices, for garnish

Serves 2 to 4

Heads will turn when you enter the room with a tray of tall glasses of this emerald-green iced tea. Your guests will love the snappy mint flavor, and the electric color suggests that this is one very refreshing beverage. Serve in frosted glasses with sprigs of fresh mint, or rub the rims of clear champagne flutes with a slice of lemon and carefully dip the rims into a saucer of sugar before filling the flutes with the tea.

**1.** Mix the chilled green tea with the green mint syrup and lemon juice in a medium-size pitcher.

**2.** Pour the tea mixture into tall frosted glasses filled with cracked ice. Garnish with fresh mint and lemon slices. Serve immediately.

# jasmine tea limeade

One 11-ounce can frozen limeade concentrate, diluted with 2 cans cold water

2 cups chilled jasmine tea

3 tablespoons freshly squeezed lime juice

6 tablespoons sugar

2 teaspoons lime zest

Small lemon wedge

Ice cubes

Small lime wedges or lime slices, for garnish

Serves 2 to 4

On a sultry summer night, treat your guests to the cooling effects of this Asian hot-weather rescue. This seemingly simple combination of two disparate flavors is a delicious example of how opposites attract: the heady, floral nectar of the jasmine tea adds a sweet touch to the tartness of the lime, without diminishing the charm of either flavor. Serve with thin slices of fresh, seasonal melon and papaya.

**1.** Put the limeade concentrate mixture into a medium-size pitcher and stir until thawed and blended. Add the chilled jasmine tea and lime juice and mix thoroughly.

**2.** Put the sugar on a saucer and add the lime zest. Blend well. Run the lemon wedge lightly around the rims of the glasses and carefully dip each rim into the sugar mixture.

**3.** Fill the glasses with ice and pour the tea mixture into the glasses, being careful not to disturb the sugared rims. In each glass, float 4 lime wedges or add a skewer threaded with lime slices. Serve immediately.

# in-the-pink
## iced green tea

I have always been fond of the tart delicious-
ness of fresh grapefruit and look forward to
the time of year when piles of juicy ruby-red
grapefruits from Texas and Florida appear
at the market. In my household, we not only
feast on pink grapefruit for breakfast but
add sections to fruit salads for a burst of
clean, tangy flavor. Believe it or not, green
tea and pink grapefruit create a refreshing
harmony of flavors, offering yet another way
to savor the puckery tartness of these citrus
beauties.

2 cups freshly squeezed
   pink grapefruit juice
3 cups chilled green tea
2 tablespoons light brown
   sugar
Ice cubes
Maraschino cherries,
   for garnish

Serves 2 to 4

**1.** Combine the grapefruit juice, chilled green
tea, and brown sugar in a medium-size pitcher
and stir until blended.
**2.** Pour the tea mixture into tall glasses filled
with ice cubes. Make a garnish for each glass
by sliding 1 or 2 maraschino cherries onto a
skewer. Place a skewer in each glass and serve
immediately.

For a sweeter flavor,
add a splash of cherry
or strawberry syrup
when mixing the juice,
tea, and sugar in the
pitcher.

# minty green tea lemonade

One 11-ounce can frozen
   lemonade concentrate,
   diluted with 1 can cold
   water

½ cup tightly packed fresh
   mint leaves

2 tablespoons sugar

3 tablespoons freshly
   squeezed lemon juice

2 cups chilled green tea

Ice cubes

Sprigs of fresh mint,
   for garnish

Serves 2 to 4

Lemonade and fresh mint have a natural affinity that makes them a classic combination. The addition of green tea adds another great layer of flavor. Sometimes the synergy of a flavor combination is greater than the sum of its individual ingredients—an appropriate concept for this iced tea. To ensure the best flavor, you must use fresh mint, which is available year round in the produce section of your supermarket. If you wish to juice lemons and make your lemonade from scratch, your efforts will be well rewarded.

**1.** Put the lemonade concentrate mixture into a medium-size pitcher and stir until thawed and blended.

**2.** In a 4-cup glass measuring cup, bruise the mint leaves with the sugar and lemon juice, using a wooden spoon. Add the chilled green tea. Stir to mix well, then let the flavors meld for 10 minutes.

**3.** Strain the tea mixture into the pitcher with the lemonade and stir well.

**4.** Pour the tea-lemonade mixture into tall glasses filled with ice. Garnish with mint sprigs and serve immediately.

# toasted coconut iced green tea

You will impress your most discriminating friends with this sophisticated iced tea. Besides its surprising, elegant white color and slightly creamy texture, this iced tea has the additional twist of subtle tropical flavor. Genmaicha is a specialty Japanese tea that has tiny kernels of toasted rice mixed in with the green tea leaf. The delicate and subtle flavor of the toasted rice underscores the richness of the coconut, creating an intriguing and delicious iced tea.

One 10-ounce can frozen piña colada cocktail mix (non-alcoholic)

4 cups chilled Genmaicha tea

Ice cubes

Fresh pineapple wedges, for garnish

Serves 2 to 4

**1.** Put the piña colada cocktail mix into a medium-size pitcher and add the tea. Stir until thawed and blended.

**2.** Pour the tea mixture into old-fashioned glasses filled with ice. Garnish each glass with a fresh pineapple wedge and serve immediately.

# green tea, pear, and almond horchata

This pale ivory–colored breakfast smoothie was inspired by beverages that I discovered in Mexico. Horchatas are made by blending uncooked rice or nuts with fruit and dairy; this gives them a grainy, slightly thickened texture. For this smoothie, I use blanched almonds to complement the subtle sweetness of the pear and give this drink the traditional graininess.

Place all of the ingredients in a blender, adding the ice cubes last. Blend for 2 to 3 minutes at medium speed, or until the ice is completely crushed and incorporated. Pour into glasses and serve immediately.

1 cup chilled green tea

½ cup regular or low-fat plain yogurt

½ cup natural pear juice or nectar

1 medium-size ripe pear, cored, peeled, and quartered

1 ripe banana, peeled and quartered

10 seedless white grapes, halved

3 tablespoons slivered or sliced raw blanched almonds

4 ice cubes

Serves 2 to 4

# pineapple-apricot green tea smoothie

½ cup chilled green tea

1 cup regular or low-fat plain yogurt

2 cups chopped fresh or canned pineapple

1 cup peeled and quartered apricots

1 medium-size navel orange, peeled, pith removed, and chopped

4 ice cubes

Serves 2 to 4

This smoothie features a truly delicious combination of flavors. If you are feeling ambitious, peel, pit, and bake the apricots cut-side up in a baking dish at 350°F for 35 minutes. Roasting the apricots will soften them and intensify their flavor, creating a sensational taste combination with the pineapple.

Place all of the ingredients in a blender, adding the ice cubes last. Blend for 2 to 3 minutes at medium speed, or until the ice is completely crushed and incorporated. Pour into glasses and serve immediately.

# cherry green tea smoothie

The color-rich team of black cherry juice and black cherry yogurt give this smoothie a striking color. For the best flavor, use all-natural, sugar-free pure black cherry juice and ripe, local red raspberries. When raspberries are out of season, use whole, individually quick frozen (IQF), no-sugar-added raspberries, which are available in soft-pack pouches at your supermarket.

Place all of the ingredients in a blender, adding the ice cubes last. Blend for 2 to 3 minutes on medium speed, or until the ice is completely crushed and incorporated. Pour into glasses and serve immediately.

½ cup chilled green tea

One 6-ounce container regular or low-fat black cherry yogurt

½ cup natural black cherry juice

1 ripe banana, peeled and quartered

1 cup fresh or frozen raspberries

1 tablespoon honey

4 ice cubes

Serves 2 to 4

# green tea apricot-mango smoothie

1 cup chilled green tea

1 cup regular or low-fat plain yogurt

1 cup mango puree

1 cup peeled and quartered fresh apricots

4 ice cubes

Serves 2 to 4

Blessed with a bright tropical color, this smoothie is a great eye-opener. I use Mira brand ready-to-use mango puree, available in Tetra Paks at your local Asian market. Or you can use canned sliced mangoes with excellent results. Just drain the slices (reserve the juice for another purpose), then puree the fruit. This is also an easy and delicious way to obtain mango puree for making sorbet or ice cream.

Place all of the ingredients in a blender, adding the ice cubes last. Blend for 2 to 3 minutes at medium speed, or until the ice is completely crushed and incorporated. Pour into glasses and serve immediately.

# no-moo red-on-red green tea smoothie

½ cup chilled green tea

1 cup silken tofu

½ cup natural peach juice

1 cup fresh strawberries

½ cup fresh raspberries

1 medium-size fresh peach, peeled, pitted, and quartered

1 teaspoon honey

4 ice cubes

Serves 2 to 4

The combination of raspberries and strawberries is an American summer classic. For this nondairy smoothie, look for Mori-Nu brand silken tofu, which comes in little red-and-white boxes. It has a fine, creamy texture and a light, subtle flavor that will complement, not overwhelm, the rest of the ingredients. Also, it is made from GMO-free soybeans.

Place all of the ingredients in a blender, adding the ice cubes last. Blend for 2 to 3 minutes at medium speed, or until the ice is completely crushed and incorporated. Pour into glasses and serve immediately.

**This is at its best when the fruits are in season, but in a pinch you can use whole, individually quick frozen (IQF) berries and canned, water-packed peaches.**

# green tea, watermelon, and pear smoothie

Delicately pink in color, this refreshing smoothie has an intriguing flavor. Ripe honeydew or Crenshaw melon can be substituted for the watermelon, with equally delicious results. Matcha powder is made from shade-grown Japanese green tea leaves that have been ground to a powdery consistency.

**1.** Put the yogurt into a small dish and carefully whisk in the matcha powder in small amounts until smooth and fully incorporated.

**2.** Put the yogurt mixture into a blender along with the chilled green tea, pears, and watermelon. Add the ice cubes and blend for 2 to 3 minutes at medium speed, or until the ice is completely crushed and incorporated. Pour into glasses and serve immediately.

1 cup regular or low-fat plain yogurt

2 teaspoons matcha powder

½ cup chilled green tea

2 medium-size ripe pears, cored, peeled, and quartered

2 heaping cups chopped seedless watermelon

4 ice cubes

Serves 2 to 4

Some grades of matcha are reserved for use in the Japanese tea ceremony, while others are used for more casual tea drinking and for adding flavor and vivid green color to sauces and desserts. I recommend using Kiri No Ne matcha from Japan; it comes freshness-sealed in little tins. You can order it from www.cooksshophere.com.

# green tea, guava, and pineapple smoothie

½ cup chilled green tea

1 cup regular or low-fat plain yogurt

1 cup guava puree

2 cups chopped fresh or canned pineapple

1 medium-size apple, cored, peeled, and quartered

4 ice cubes

Serves 2 to 4

I love the unabashed lusciousness of guava, with its sublime, sweet flavor and intense pink color. Here, the rich sweetness of guava flirts deliciously with the tart sweetness of fresh pineapple, creating a seductive combination. While ripe, fragrant guavas can be hard to find, guava puree is readily available at Latin and Asian markets and at large supermarkets. Keep several boxes on hand, as it is excellent for both concocting drinks and making tropical fruit sauces and sorbets.

Place all of the ingredients in a blender, adding the ice cubes last. Blend for 2 to 3 minutes at medium speed, or until the ice is completely crushed and incorporated. Pour into glasses and serve immediately.

# green tea banana split smoothie

If you have a hankering for chocolate, then this recipe will speak your language. You can either be virtuous by making this with yogurt or go all out and treat yourself by using ice cream. The banana adds texture and creaminess and, of course, that ice-cream-sundae flavor. Serve this with a straw and a maraschino cherry!

Place all of the ingredients in a blender, adding the ice cubes last. Blend for 2 to 3 minutes at medium speed, or until the ice is completely crushed and incorporated. Pour into glasses and serve immediately.

½ cup chilled green tea

1 cup regular or low-fat vanilla yogurt or 1 cup vanilla ice cream

1 small ripe banana

¼ cup chocolate syrup

¼ teaspoon pure vanilla extract

4 ice cubes

Serves 2

# green tea
# cocktails

*In mixed drinks, green tea is a terrific*
replacement for juices or syrups, adding a clean, light flavor without additional sweetness or calories. With these recipes, I aimed to combine the glamour of classic drinks of yesterday with the dazzling selection of ingredients and flavors that make up today's flavor palette. Use the master recipe for Classic Iced Green Tea (page 16) to make the tea for these cocktails. Also, I recommend always pre-chilling your serving pitchers and glasses to decrease the need for ice in your drinks. This will allow the flavors to really shine. Cheers!

---

Ave Maria • Lemon Drop • Tropical Sky • Snow White • Creamsicle • Face Biter

# ave maria

4 cups cracked ice

¾ cup chilled green tea

¾ cup tequila, preferably a slightly aged, golden-colored Hornitos

¼ cup Cointreau or triple sec

6 tablespoons mango puree

2 tablespoons freshly squeezed lime juice

Lime wedges, for garnish

Serves 4

This refreshing drink is a margarita with a tropical spin. Golden-green in color, this frosty libation looks handsome in a glass and offers cooling relief on hot summer nights. Hold the salt, but do top the rim of each glass with a freshly cut lime wedge and drop in a shiny flamingo or palm tree swizzle stick just for fun! Have a fiesta and serve this with bowls of spicy guacamole or a colorful platter heaped with sliced tropical fruits.

**1.** Add the cracked ice to a large chilled pitcher. Add the green tea, tequila, Cointreau, mango puree, and lime juice. Gently swirl the pitcher to blend, then chill the mixture for 2 minutes.

**2.** Strain the cocktail into 4 margarita or old-fashioned glasses. Garnish with lime wedges and serve immediately.

# lemon drop

Along Italy's treacherous and spectacular Amalfi coast, trattorias and cafés serve icy glasses of puckery-sweet limoncello poured straight from a bottle that is kept tucked away in the freezer. Take their tip and keep your limoncello and vodka in the freezer, and have the club soda and green tea chilling in the refrigerator. If you will not be navigating the hair-raising roads of the Amalfi coast, with its endless stream of kamikaze motor scooters weaving in and out of traffic, feel free to increase the quantity of limoncello in each glass to 2 ounces. *Salute!*

4 ice cubes

3 ounces chilled green tea

1 ounce cold pepper vodka

1 ounce cold limoncello

4 to 5 teaspoons freshly squeezed lemon juice

3 ounces chilled club soda

2 lemon slices, for garnish

Serves 2

**1.** Put the ice cubes, green tea, pepper vodka, and limoncello into a large chilled pitcher. Gently swirl the pitcher to blend. Add the lemon juice to the pitcher and let the mixture chill for 2 minutes.

**2.** Strain the cocktail into 2 martini glasses. Top off the drinks with club soda and stir just to mix. Garnish each glass with a lemon slice and serve immediately.

There is also a creamy version of limoncello that you can try in this cocktail.

# tropical sky

This rosy-hued drink was inspired by the vivid red, baby-doll pink, and sun-kissed orange of a Caribbean sunrise. It is a swanky treat fit for a sophisticated evening or a celebratory brunch. Serve it in old-fashioned glasses with a cocktail skewer threaded with a maraschino cherry and wedges of lemon and orange. Dance music and bare feet are optional.

12 ice cubes

3 ounces chilled green tea

1 cup chilled pomegranate juice

3 ounces gin

1 tablespoon amaretto

Maraschino cherries, lemon wedges, and orange wedges, for garnish

Serves 2

**1.** Put 4 of the ice cubes, the green tea, pomegranate juice, gin, and amaretto into a cocktail shaker and shake vigorously for 1 minute.

**2.** Divide the remaining 8 ice cubes between 2 old-fashioned glasses. Make a skewer for each glass by threading 1 cherry, 1 lemon wedge, and 1 orange wedge onto a skewer. Strain the cocktail into the glasses and drape a fruit skewer across the top of each glass. Serve immediately.

# snow white

2 cups crushed ice

1½ cups chilled green tea

3 ounces cold vodka

1 ounce brandy

Splash of orange juice

½ cup heavy cream

2 tablespoons light brown
sugar

Matcha powder, for
garnish (see note on
page 61)

Serves 4

At first sip, this is a very romantic drink: pretty, creamy, and a bit sweet. But following its soft entrance, the brandy and vodka provide the muscular verve of a true cocktail. This drink is best served chilled when the weather is cool, with a nip of frost in the air. It is a terrific cocktail to serve with a holiday dessert buffet or after a Christmas caroling expedition.

**1.** Put the crushed ice into a blender, followed by all the remaining ingredients except the matcha powder. Blend on medium speed for 2 minutes or until all of the ice is incorporated.

**2.** Pour the cocktail into brandy snifters and dust with a touch of matcha powder. Serve immediately.

# creamsicle

One 15-ounce can cream of coconut

2 teaspoons matcha powder (see note on page 61)

One 8-ounce can mango slices, drained

¼ cup dark rum

¼ cup white port

2 cups crushed ice

½ cup club soda

Fresh pineapple spears and maraschino cherries, for garnish

Serves 2

Instead of the canned mango, you can use 8 ounces of Mira brand mango puree or slices of fresh mango.

This creamy, decadent drink is always welcome, whether served on the beach at a late summer lobster fest in Maine or while lounging poolside with the Sunday paper in Los Angeles. Be sure to use sweetened cream of coconut in this drink, rather than coconut milk. I adore the way the silky texture of mango puree combines with the cream of coconut and gives this drink a sinfully rich panache. The matcha powder adds just a wisp of color and tempers the sweetness.

**1.** Put the cream of coconut into a small bowl and carefully whisk in the matcha powder in small amounts until smooth and fully incorporated.

**2.** Pour the coconut mixture into a blender. Add the mango slices and blend until well incorporated.

**3.** Add the rum, port, and crushed ice, then blend until smooth and creamy. Add the club soda and blend just to incorporate, about 30 seconds.

**4.** Make a skewer for each glass by threading a pineapple spear and a cherry onto a skewer. Pour the cocktail into hurricane or highball glasses and garnish with the fruit skewers. Serve immediately.

For this drink I use Busha Browne's Sherry Pepper Sauce, an amber-colored, very thin hot sauce from Jamaica that has a bone-dry style and razor-sharp flavor. Made from sherry that has been macerated with fresh Scotch bonnet peppers and other spices, this sauce has a wonderful hot kick that adds spike and backbone to bar drinks. It will keep practically a lifetime in the refrigerator, so it is well worth acquiring a bottle. Tomato-based or vinegar-based hot sauces are not good substitutes for sherry pepper sauce—use a Bermuda-style sherry pepper sauce if you cannot find Busha Browne's. Can't find either? Leave it out and then you will have a Face Kisser!

16 ice cubes

1 cup chilled green tea

2 cups chilled natural pineapple juice

½ cup chilled natural pear juice or nectar

¼ cup gin

¼ cup white rum

2 teaspoons Busha Browne's Sherry Pepper Sauce

Fresh pineapple spears, for garnish

Serves 4

**1.** Add 4 of the ice cubes and all of the remaining ingredients except the pineapple spears to a large chilled pitcher. Gently swirl the pitcher to blend, then chill the mixture for 2 minutes.

**2.** Divide the remaining 12 ice cubes between 4 old-fashioned glasses. Strain the cocktail into the glasses and stand a pineapple spear in each glass. Serve immediately.

savory dishes
and sweet
endings

$\int$ n Asia, creative cooks find many ways to use green tea in everyday cooking. In addition to seasoning broths and poaching liquids, tea leaves become a vegetable in rice dishes or stir-frys and a flavoring in piquant dipping sauces and custardy desserts. Look for small containers of matcha, a silky-fine, powdered Japanese green tea, in specialty tea shops. Matcha is the key to imparting that green-tea color to food, and, once you get the feel for using it, it is easy to add a little to enhance your favorite pound cake or butter cookie recipe. Try using green tea as a seasoning and flavoring in some of your favorite dishes, and you will soon find yourself discovering new uses for this versatile flavor.

---

Green Tea–Steamed Mussels with Two Mayonnaises • Spicy Green Tea–Rubbed Salmon • Asian Shrimp Boil • Grilled Chicken Satay with Green Tea–Peanut Sauce • Crunchy Sesame Seed–Crusted Pork • Fresh Fruit Salad with Green Tea Syrup • Pears Poached in Spicy Green Tea • Green Tea–Honey Cookies • White Chocolate–Green Tea Ice Cream • Cool and Silken Green Tea–Citrus Custard

# green tea–steamed mussels with two mayonnaises

**Chipotle-Orange Mayonnaise**

¼ cup mayonnaise

1 teaspoon ground chipotle chile powder

2 tablespoons freshly squeezed orange juice

**Matcha Mayonnaise**

¼ cup mayonnaise

1 teaspoon matcha powder (see note on page 61)

Few drops lemon juice

4 tablespoons (16 grams) medium-size loose-leaf green tea or 8 green tea bags

8 cups water, heated to 175° to 180°F

One 2-inch piece peeled fresh ginger, grated

4 to 5 pounds mussels

Serves 8 as an appetizer or 4 as a main course

In this recipe, a green tea infusion tenderizes the mussels and imbues them with a rich golden-mahogany color. The tantalizingly zingy aroma of the freshly grated ginger perfumes both the mussels and your kitchen. To cook the mussels, use a large pot, a covered roasting pan, or a deep paella pan, spreading the mussels in a shallow layer over the bottom of the pan so that they can open easily.

**1.** Make the two mayonnaises, one at a time, by whisking together each batch of ingredients. Cover and refrigerate until needed.

**2.** Put the tea leaves or tea bags into a 4-cup heatproof measuring cup. Pour 4 cups of the hot water over the tea, cover with a clean kitchen towel, and brew for 2 minutes.

**3.** Strain the brewed tea into a large pot. Infuse the tea a second time, in the same manner, with the remaining 4 cups water, and add this tea to the pot. Add the ginger to the brewed tea in the pot. Mix well.

**4.** Place the mussels in a large bowl and cover with water. Discard any that are cracked or broken. Gently stir the mussels to wash them, and scrub any that need cleaning. Change the water as necessary until the mussels are clean. Discard any mussels that remain open and have not closed tightly. If any of the mussels has a hairy

beard, grab the beard near the base of the shell and remove it with a firm tug. Drain the mussels.

**5.** Bring the tea to a simmer over medium-high heat and add the mussels, spreading them evenly over the bottom of the pot. Cover tightly and simmer for 5 minutes. Remove the lid and carefully shift the mussels around with a wooden spoon. If necessary, cover and continue cooking for a few more minutes, until all the mussels have opened. Discard any that do not.

**6.** With a slotted spoon, remove the mussels to a serving bowl. Ladle a generous amount of the cooking liquid over them. Serve with hot crusty bread and pass bowls of the two mayonnaises for dipping or stirring into the broth.

 Mussels are so versatile and are a wonderful canvas for your culinary creativity. Here they are given an Asian preparation, but in Normandy, France, restaurants serve up earthy and delicious plates of steaming mussels that have been cooked in locally produced hard cider and rich cream.

# spicy green tea-rubbed salmon

These salmon steaks are savory and succulent. The aromatic spice rub adds a sultry, mysterious flavor to the fish, along with some texture. For the salt in this rub I like to use Maldon crystals from England, which have a clean, briny flavor.

1. To make the spice rub, put the tea leaves into a mortar and, using a straight up-and-down motion, strike the leaves with the pestle to crush them. One spice at a time, add the Szechuan peppercorns, grains of paradise, and green peppercorns to the mortar, crushing each with the same up-and-down motion. Add the salt last, then gently mix to blend all the spices together. Set aside.

2. Heat a large frying pan, stovetop grill, or outdoor grill until very hot.

3. Brush the salmon lightly with canola oil. Press some of the spice rub onto one side of the fish until well covered.

4. Spread a little oil over the pan or grill to prevent the fish from sticking. Gently place the salmon in the pan or on the grill with the spice-rub side facing up and cook for about 5 minutes, without lifting or turning.

5. Carefully flip the salmon so that the spice-rub side is facing down and continue to cook for 5 more minutes, or until the salmon is opaque and flaky. Remove from the heat and serve immediately.

**Spicy Green Tea Rub**

3 tablespoons (12 grams) loose-leaf green tea

1 teaspoon Szechuan peppercorns

1 teaspoon grains of paradise

1 teaspoon dry (not in brine) green peppercorns

1 teaspoon coarse sea salt

Four 1-inch-thick salmon fillets or steaks (6 to 8 ounces each)

Canola oil

Serves 4

Grains of paradise, or Melegueta pepper, are tiny round black seeds from a plant in the same family as ginger and cardamom.

# asian shrimp boil

2 tablespoons (8 grams) loose-leaf Genmaicha tea

4 cups water, boiled and cooled to 175° to 180°F

One 5-inch cinnamon stick, broken in half

5 whole star anise

2 tablespoons whole black peppercorns

1 tablespoon whole fennel seeds

1 tablespoon red pepper flakes

2 teaspoons salt

2 tablespoons Asian hot chile paste

1 tablespoon Worcestershire sauce

¼ cup soy sauce

One 2-inch piece peeled fresh ginger, cut into 6 slices

Six ¼-inch-thick slices lemon

¼ cup freshly squeezed orange juice

1 pound medium-size shrimp (36 to 40 per pound), peeled and deveined

Serves 4 as an appetizer

Serve hot bowls of this delicious shrimp at your next party and watch it disappear. Simple to prepare and a snap to cook, this Asian variation of a Louisiana shrimp boil requires virtually no advance prep. Just raid your spice drawer and you are ready to cook. The toasty Genmaicha tea plays nicely to the sweetness of the shrimp. Provide guests with colorful cocktail picks or forks and plenty of napkins.

**1.** Put the tea leaves into a 4-cup heatproof measuring cup. Pour the water over the tea and brew for 2 minutes. Strain the brewed tea into a large pot.

**2.** Add all the remaining ingredients except for the shrimp to the brewed tea and bring the mixture to a simmer over medium heat. Add the shrimp, increasing the heat just a bit, but do not boil. Cook the shrimp for 3 minutes, or until they turn pink.

**3.** Remove the pot from the heat. With a slotted spoon, lift out the shrimp and as much of the spice mixture as you can, and place it all in a shallow serving bowl.

**4.** Add about ½ cup of the cooking liquid to the shrimp in the bowl. Mix the spices and the shrimp together well and serve immediately.

# grilled chicken satay with green tea–peanut sauce

For maximum flavor in this dish, I recommend that you marinate the chicken for 2 hours before grilling in a mixture of equal parts soy sauce, Thai fish sauce, peanut oil, rice vinegar, and lime juice. You need a total of about 1 cup of liquid (about 3 tablespoons of each ingredient). Accompany this dish with jasmine rice, sliced cucumbers tossed with vinegar, and fresh pineapple wedges.

**1.** Place all the sauce ingredients in the work bowl of a food processor or blender and puree. Let the mixture sit for 30 minutes at room temperature to let the flavors blend.

**2.** Prepare a hot fire in your grill, or heat a stovetop grill.

**3.** Thread the chicken onto the skewers and grill for 10 to 15 minutes, turning once. Be careful not to overcook the meat. To serve, stack the skewers on a platter and pass bowls of the peanut sauce for drizzling.

**Green Tea–Peanut Sauce**

¼ cup smooth peanut butter

1 tablespoon soy sauce

2 tablespoons rice vinegar

2 tablespoons toasted sesame oil

1 teaspoon hot chile oil

2 teaspoons freshly squeezed lime juice

2 tablespoons light brown sugar

2 teaspoons peeled and finely minced fresh ginger

2 tablespoons finely minced previously brewed green tea leaves

2 pounds boneless chicken breasts, thinly sliced lengthwise

Bamboo skewers, soaked in water for 30 minutes

Serves 4

You can substitute thinly sliced pork or beef or peeled and deveined shrimp for the chicken.

# crunchy sesame seed-crusted pork

2 tablespoons soy sauce

2 tablespoons rice vinegar

1 tablespoon toasted sesame oil

2 tablespoons Asian hot chile paste

Two 12-ounce pork tenderloins

1 teaspoon Szechuan peppercorns

1 tablespoon (4 grams) medium-size loose-leaf green tea

1 tablespoon brown sesame seeds

1 tablespoon black sesame seeds

1 tablespoon coarse sea salt

1½ teaspoons Chinese five-spice powder

2 tablespoons light brown sugar

Serves 4

Use small pork tenderloins for this recipe, and roast them quickly at a high temperature to keep them tender and juicy. Rolling the cooked pork in the spice mixture *after* taking it out of the oven keeps the coating crunchy.

**1.** Preheat the oven to 450°F.

**2.** Mix the soy sauce, vinegar, sesame oil, and chile paste in an 11 x 9-inch baking dish. Add the pork and turn to coat all sides.

**3.** Roast the pork for about 20 minutes, turning once, until an instant-read thermometer inserted into the thickest part of the roast registers 150°F. Remove the pork from the oven and transfer to a platter to rest for 5 minutes.

**4.** While the pork is roasting, lightly crush the peppercorns and green tea using a mortar and pestle. Add the sesame seeds, salt, five-spice powder, and brown sugar and stir to blend well. Spread the spice mixture on a large plate.

**5.** Using tongs, roll the pork in the spice mixture to cover completely. Return to the platter, slice, and serve immediately.

# fresh fruit salad with green tea syrup

Feel free to use whatever fruits are available, depending on the time of year when you make this. It's hard to go wrong with fruit salad combinations. Serve this plain, or add a dollop of plain yogurt, mascarpone cheese, or whipped cream to each serving.

1. Put the brewed tea, sugar, honey, lemon juice, and mint leaves in a small saucepan and heat over medium heat, stirring occasionally, until the sugar and honey dissolve. Simmer for 2 minutes, then remove from the heat and pour the syrup into a heatproof bowl to cool. Remove and discard the mint leaves.

2. Cut the skin off the grapefruit and other citrus fruits and cut into sections. Halve the apple and the pear, remove each core, and cut into cubes. Leave the grapes whole or halve them.

3. Place all the fruit in a large serving bowl and drizzle the cooled green tea syrup over it. Mix gently to blend and let sit for 30 minutes, either at room temperature or in the refrigerator. Just before serving, mix gently again.

½ cup brewed green tea

¼ cup sugar

1 tablespoon mild floral honey, such as tupelo, raspberry, or lavender

1 tablespoon freshly squeezed lemon juice

6 large fresh mint leaves

1 large grapefruit

4 assorted orange citrus fruits, such as navel or blood oranges, mineolas, clementines, or tangelos

1 medium-size apple

1 medium-size pear

1 cup whole seedless red or green grapes

Serves 4

You can make the green tea syrup a day ahead, if you wish.

# pears poached in spicy green tea

The spicy poaching liquid in this dish has a tantalizing sweet-tart flavor, and is an upbeat variation on the usual wine-based poaching liquid. Use any firm green pears, such as Anjou, Bartlett, Comice, or Magness. Serve these warm from the stovetop or make them ahead and serve chilled. For a beautiful presentation, place each pear in a shallow bowl and serve accompanied by whipped cream dusted with matcha powder, or with a scoop of White Chocolate–Green Tea Ice Cream (page 88).

4 cups water

2 tablespoons (8 grams) medium-size loose-leaf green tea or 4 green tea bags

1 tablespoon whole black peppercorns

8 large slices peeled fresh ginger

1 cup unfiltered apple cider

4 slices lemon

6 whole white cardamom pods

4 whole star anise

6 whole cloves

Two 5-inch cinnamon sticks

½ cup Campari or pomegranate juice

4 whole ripe pears

Serves 4

1. Put all the ingredients except the pears into a large saucepan. Mix well, then bring to a simmer over medium heat.

2. Peel the pears, leaving the stems attached as well as a little peel around the stems. Trim the bottoms as needed to give the pears a flat base.

3. When the poaching liquid is simmering, add the pears and simmer for 10 to 20 minutes, depending on the size of the pears. The pears should be soft but not overcooked; check for doneness by inserting the tip of a paring knife into the pears.

4. Allow the pears to cool in the poaching liquid. Remove the pears and arrange on a serving platter.

# green tea–honey cookies

2 cups all-purpose flour

½ teaspoon ground cloves

1 teaspoon ground cinnamon

1 cup sliced blanched almonds

1 cup (2 sticks) unsalted butter

1 cup sugar

2 large eggs, well beaten

1½ cups wildflower honey

2 tablespoons Sencha tea

**Makes about 40 cookies**

**Instead of parchment paper, you can also use silicone baking sheet liners (such as Silpat brand) to keep the cookies from sticking to the pan.**

Thin and crisp, these cookies are perfect with an afternoon cup of green tea. I like to use Japanese Sencha tea, which has long, needle-shaped leaves. It holds its shape during baking and adds beautiful forest green slashes of color to the cookies. The dough will spread during baking, so be sure to leave plenty of room between the cookies on the baking sheet.

**1.** Preheat the oven to 350°F. Line 4 baking sheets with parchment paper.

**2.** Mix the flour, cloves, cinnamon, and almonds in a large bowl. In another large bowl, use an electric mixer to cream the butter until fluffy. Add the sugar, beaten eggs, and honey, and beat until the mixture is smooth. Add the flour mixture to the butter mixture in several batches, blending completely after each addition. Add the Sencha and blend just to incorporate.

**3.** Drop generous teaspoons of cookie dough onto the prepared baking sheets, leaving 2 inches between cookies. Bake for 15 to 17 minutes, or until the cookies are a rich golden color.

**4.** Remove the cookies from the oven, let sit for 1 minute on the baking sheets, and then carefully transfer them to a cooling rack to cool completely. The cookies will keep for several days in an airtight container.

# white chocolate–green tea ice cream

8 ounces high-quality white chocolate, chopped into ½-inch pieces

2 cups light cream

1 cup heavy cream

1 teaspoon pure vanilla extract

5 large egg yolks, at room temperature

¾ cup packed light brown sugar

2 tablespoons matcha powder (see note on page 61)

Makes 1 quart

This velvety, custard-style ice cream is the epitome of serene cool. The brown sugar and white chocolate combine to create a rich background for the flavor of the matcha powder, which also lends a lively green color. If you wish, accompany this ice cream with delicate almond tuile cookies or ultra-thin ginger wafers.

**1.** Place the white chocolate pieces in a large heatproof bowl. Set aside.

**2.** Combine the light cream, heavy cream, and vanilla extract in a medium-size saucepan. Over medium heat, bring the mixture just to a boil, stirring constantly. Remove from the heat and set aside.

**3.** In a large bowl, whisk the yolks until well blended. In a small bowl, blend the brown sugar with the matcha powder until there are no green streaks, then whisk the sugar mixture into the egg yolks, blending well.

**4.** Add ¼ cup of the hot cream mixture to the egg mixture, whisking vigorously. Add another ¼ cup and whisk again. Carefully pour this mixture back into the saucepan, mix well, and cook over medium heat until the custard is thick enough to coat the back of a spoon, about 170°F. Do not boil, or the custard will curdle.

**5.** Remove the custard from the heat and strain through a fine-mesh strainer into the bowl of chopped white chocolate. Stir until the chocolate is completely melted, then let the custard cool at room temperature for 15 minutes.

**6.** Cover the custard and chill in the refrigerator for 6 hours or overnight. Freeze in an ice cream machine according to the manufacturer's instructions. Transfer the ice cream to an airtight container and place in the freezer until firm, at least 8 hours. Remove from the freezer 20 minutes before serving.

# cool and silken green tea–citrus custard

On a tea-buying trip to western China, I jumped at the chance to stop in Cambodia and explore the awe-inspiring ancient temple complex of Angkor Wat. At the historic Raffles Grand Hotel d'Angkor in Siem Reap, I swooned over a delicate custard redolent of tropical fruit flavors and aromas. Here is my version. Unlike traditional custards, this one has a minimum of cream for a lighter, fresher style. It is pleasingly moss-green in color, and, because it is not baked, it is perfect for presenting in an assortment of your most fanciful small and stylish bowls.

¼ cup (½ stick) unsalted butter

¾ cup sugar

1½ teaspoons matcha powder (see note on page 61)

⅔ cup apricot nectar

2 teaspoons unflavored gelatin

½ cup heavy cream

½ cup freshly squeezed orange juice

4 large eggs, lightly beaten

Serves 6

**1.** Fill the bottom of a double boiler with water to ¾ inch below the bottom of the top pan. Bring the water to a boil, then turn off the heat. Place the butter in the top pan of the double boiler. Once it has melted, remove the top pan and place it on a heatproof pad on the countertop.

**2.** Mix the sugar and the matcha powder in a small bowl until well blended. Add the sugar mixture to the melted butter and blend well. Set aside.

**3.** Put the apricot nectar into a small bowl and sprinkle the gelatin over it to soften. Set aside.

**4.** Add the cream, orange juice, and beaten eggs to the butter mixture. Blend to incorporate well. Place the pan back over the hot water in the bottom of the double boiler. Cook the mixture over low heat, stirring constantly, for 5 to 7 minutes, or until the mixture thickens enough to coat the back of a spoon. Be careful to not let the mixture boil, or it will curdle.

**5.** Remove the custard from the heat and strain through a fine-mesh strainer into a bowl. Add the apricot mixture to the custard and stir well, until the gelatin is dissolved and well incorporated. Allow the custard to cool at room temperature for 30 minutes. Pour the custard into 6 small ramekins or bowls, cover, and refrigerate for at least 4 hours or overnight, until set. Serve chilled.

# resource guide

**Culinary Specialties CooksShopHere**
www.cooksshophere.com
*Chinese and Japanese green teas, spices, dried flowers, sugars; tea paraphernalia and brewing equipment*

**Harney & Sons**
www.harney.com
*Chinese and Japanese green teas*

**Imperial Tea Court**
www.imperialtea.com
*Chinese green teas*

**Ito En**
www.itoen.com
*Japanese green teas*

**Peet's Coffee & Tea**
www.peets.com
*Chinese and Japanese green teas*

**Simpson & Vail**
www.svtea.com
*Chinese and Japanese green teas*

**Stash Tea**
www.stashtea.com
*Chinese and Japanese green teas*

**Ten Tea Company**
www.tentea.com
*Chinese and Japanese green teas*

**Upton Tea Imports**
www.uptontea.com
*Chinese and Japanese green teas*

**Mark T. Wendell Co.**
www.marktwendell.com
*Chinese and Japanese green teas*

# measurement equivalents

| Liquid Conversions | | Weight Conversions | | Oven Temperature Conversions | | |
|---|---|---|---|---|---|---|
| U.S. | Metric | U.S. | Metric | °F | Gas Mark | °C |
| 1 tsp | 5 ml | ½ oz | 14 g | 250 | ½ | 120 |
| 1 tbs | 5 ml | 1 oz | 28 g | 275 | 1 | 140 |
| 2 tbs | 30 ml | 1½ oz | 43 g | 300 | 2 | 150 |
| 3 tbs | 45 ml | 2 oz | 57 g | 325 | 3 | 165 |
| ¼ cup | 60 ml | 2½ oz | 71 g | 350 | 4 | 180 |
| ⅓ cup | 75 ml | 3 oz | 85 g | 375 | 5 | 190 |
| ⅓ cup + 1 tbs | 90 ml | 3½ oz | 100 g | 400 | 6 | 200 |
| ⅓ cup + 2 tbs | 100 ml | 4 oz | 113 g | 425 | 7 | 220 |
| ½ cup | 120 ml | 5 oz | 142 g | 450 | 8 | 230 |
| ⅔ cup | 150 ml | 6 oz | 170 g | 475 | 9 | 240 |
| ¾ cup | 180 ml | 7 oz | 200 g | 500 | 10 | 260 |
| ¾ cup + 2 tbs | 200 ml | 8 oz | 227 g | 550 | Broil | 290 |
| 1 cup | 240 ml | 9 oz | 255 g | | | |
| 1 cup + 2 tbs | 275 ml | 10 oz | 284 g | | | |
| 1¼ cups | 300 ml | 11 oz | 312 g | | | |
| 1⅓ cups | 325 ml | 12 oz | 340 g | | | |
| 1½ cups | 350 ml | 13 oz | 368 g | | | |
| 1⅔ cups | 375 ml | 14 oz | 400 g | | | |
| 1¾ cups | 400 ml | 15 oz | 425 g | | | |
| 1¾ cups + 2 tbs | 450 ml | 1 lb | 454 g | | | |
| 2 cups (1 pint) | 475 ml | | | | | |
| 2½ cups | 600 ml | | | | | |
| 3 cups | 720 ml | | | | | |
| 4 cups (1 quart) | 945 ml | | | | | |
| (1,000 ml is 1 liter) | | | | | | |

*Please note that all conversions are approximate.*

# index

# index

# about the author

Mary Lou Heiss is a food and travel writer who loves all things Asian and European. She is co-owner of and specialty foods buyer for Culinary Specialties Cooks-ShopHere, a gourmet food shop in Northampton, Massachusetts, that she and her husband founded 30 years ago. Visit www.cooksshophere.com, her store's Web site, for photographs and information gathered from her frequent tea-sourcing trips to Asia. Mary Lou Heiss lives in western Massachusetts.